THIS BOOK IS AUTOGRAPHED
For
LORIE

D1316726

This book was written to:

1. Motivate you to work hard to achieve your dreams.
2. Inspire you and teach you how to stay focused on task.
3. Teach you how to be determined to succeed in life.

Dear Lorl,
You can achieve anything
in AMERICA if you
believe in yourself, work
hard with determination.
Live your DREAM.
AZuka 2/

# REVIEWS FOR
# THE 8 SUCCESS SECRETS FOR TEENS
# AND YOUNG ADULTS

You have definitely achieved your objective of creating a self-help book for teens and young adults. Readers will be inspired and encouraged to work hard at achieving all of their dreams and goals.

Your book is structured in a logical manner, starting with your (and your readers') beginnings and ending with a set of affirmations for your readers to continue repeating even after they finish reading your book. The activities at the end of each chapter will be useful for readers to apply your concepts to their own lives.

The tone and style of your manuscript are very age appropriate for your intended audience. The short sentences and occasional use of bulleted lists make the book easy to read and comprehend.

Your overall tone is uplifting and empowering. You tell enough success stories that readers will see that hard work and education are the keys to success.

Overall, the manuscript was in good grammatical shape.

-Maria, Editor, at Amazon Group.

Praise from Teens and Young Adults Who Read This Book.

*Thank you Azuka for writing this book. I only talk to the kids that are smart and want to learn more. You reminded me that I can work hard to become anything I want in my life. I am reading more now. Thank you so much.*

-Alyssa Billups, 8 years old.
West End School,
North Plainfield, New Jersey.

*This book is very powerful and you have inspired me to work hard to become an author when I grow up so that I can write to teach other teens and the youth how to be successful in life like you. There are three things I like about this book. The first one is that this book made me to believe that I can be very successful. It made me believe that I can be a straight "A's" student. Finally this book motivates me to live my dream. Thank you so much for giving me this book.*

-Aaron Nazaire, 11 years old.
Burnet Middle School,
Union, New Jersey.

*As a freshman in College, this book is an inspiration for young adults like me. It taught me to stay focused on my goals, to believe, to dream, to be confident and to be proud of myself. It also taught me to reach for my best because every human being is endowed with divine energy, abundance of innate resources and has the power to reach for greater heights. I learnt from this book that the sky is the limit if you are willing to try.*

-Sebastien Vladimir Dosmas, 18 years old.
Union County College,
New Jersey.

*This book teaches young ones like me a way of life they usually don't think about. It allowed me for one to open up my mind to see how harsh the world really is and that I need to prepare myself for it. I recommended this book to everyone I associate with, because it is a real eye opener.*

-Leanna Billups, 14 years old.
North Plainfield High School,
North Plainfield, New Jersey.

*I am eleven years old. The first thing I like about this book is that it gives kids opportunity to learn how to change their lives. The book taught me how to focus on my studies and also do my homework so that I can get good grades in school. The second thing I like about this book is that it motivates people to tap into their talents, follow their dreams to be successful in life.*

-Matthew Nazaire, 11 years old.
Burnet Middle School,
Union, New Jersey.

*When I received this book, I was so happy to learn that you are the author. This book taught me that if I work hard with determination I will be successful in life. Thank you Dad, for writing this book for young people like me. I am so proud of you.*

-Chidalu "Nana" Obi, 12 years old.
St. Anthony's Academy,
Anambra State.
Nigeria, West Africa.

*This book is really helping me in my life as a teenager. It taught me that I should listen to my Mom more even when she tells me to do my chores. I now listen and obey my Mom because I know she loves me and wants the best for me. Thank you Azuka Zuke for writing this book.*

-Saniah Billups, 11 years old.
Somerset School,
North Plainfield, New Jersey.

*Your book "The 8 Success Secrets for Teens and Young Adults" is really inspiring. I often forget that to get to where you want to be in life, it takes hard work and dedication. This book has reminded me of that.*

-Brittney Benjamin, 15 years old.
Saint Vincent's Academy,
Newark, New Jersey.

*This book has changed the way I see life and have taught me that the only way to a better life is to work hard with determination and faith in myself. Now I know better.*

-Ebuka "Ebuks" Onwukwe, 26 years old.
College Student,
Anambra State, Nigeria.

# THE 8 SUCCESS SECRETS FOR TEENS AND YOUNG ADULTS

# THE 8 SUCCESS SECRETS FOR TEENS AND YOUNG ADULTS

## Azuka Zuke Obi

**Author of The Power to Excel**

ISBN: 151689832X
ISBN 13: 9781516898329
Library of Congress Control Number: 2015915164
CreateSpace Independent Publishing Platform
North Charleston, South Carolina

# THE 8 SUCCESS SECRETS

1. A GOOD START
2. LISTEN TO YOUR PARENTS AND SENIORS
3. WORK VERY HARD
4. SHARPEN YOUR MORAL VALUES
5. GET DAILY EXERCISE
6. BE NICE TO PEOPLE—VOLUNTEER
7. BE THANKFUL EVERY DAY
8. YOU CAN BE ANYTHING YOU WANT- BELIEVE IT

*Dear Azuka,*

*Together, let's always remember to guard against cynicism, embrace hope, and work toward an ever brighter tomorrow.*
*I wish you all the best.*

*-President Barack Obama*
*(from a letter to the author dated April 9, 2015)*

# BELIEVE IN YOURSELF

Create a strong and unshakable belief in yourself and in your dreams. Hold them to your heart. Your dreams belong to you. It's your birthright. Never let anyone tell you that you can't achieve anything *big*. If people tell you this, just say, "Watch me, and see what I will be in the future." Then move on, and keep working toward your dreams. Observe more, talk less, listen more, ask questions, and think through the answers. Read, learn all you can, and commit to doing something new every day. I urge you to work hard toward creating a successful life starting now you're young.  Keep your eyes on the big stuff at all times. Stay away from people who gossip all the time discussing nonsense that does not benefit you in any way. Stay focused on doing the right thing every single day. Stay positive by reading good books that teaches you how to make positive changes in your life. Read one positive book every month and practice what you read. If you do, with time it becomes part of you and you will learn so much that your life will be powerful. You can do this. Yes you can.

In this book, you'll learn how to apply the positive steps to help shape your life in the right direction. You will learn how to apply simple moral values to your life to create the great person you were meant to be. You will learn how to manage your time well, seek for help, support and learn how to find your calling to ignite the genius in you which ordinarily would've been lying dormant. This short volume will help you define who you are and will change your life forever.

Understand this: if you block every distraction and put in your best with confidence and faith in yourself and in what you do, you'll be successful. Just believe it, follow your passion and keep working towards your dreams. Guess what, I am rooting for you.

-Azuka, a disciple of the movement for positive change and gratitude.

# MY DEFINITION OF
# SUCCESS FOR *YOU*

*Sometimes you win, and sometimes you lose, but never give up.*
*Unthankful hearts are losers; be grateful and thankful every day.*
*Constantly take positive actions, for actions bring results.*
*Celebrate every single day, because it's a blessing and a miracle.*
*Envisage the future you want for yourself always, because it's possible.*
*Search for new knowledge every single day, be a perpetual student.*
*Start creating your future now that you are young, strong, and very active.*

Signed *Lorie Leroy*

Date *2/06/16*

By signing and dating this definition, you hold yourself accountable to succeed. Now photocopy this page and place it at a location where you can read it every morning and before retiring to bed at night. Read it, practice the definitions and with time, you will have memorized it and can recite it by heart. When you say something out loud and feel what you say, there is a force that attracts those things into your life if you believe them with all your heart. It's like praying and believing strongly that your prayers will be answered. Your success in life begins with making good choices. To succeed in and out of the classroom, you need a positive attitude. You need to focus on your goals and learn to manage your time well while working hard to make the best use of the opportunities around you. In your hands lies a book that'll help you learn how to be outstanding and become a successful person starting now that you are young. Underline and highlight everything that seems important to you as you read this book. Make it your best friend and you'll be on the way to creating a great future.

# TABLE OF CONTENTS

# DEDICATION

To Chidalu "Nana" Obi, my son, for motivating me to write a book that teaches teens and young adults how to aim for success in life To the Roselle Public Library, Roselle, New Jersey, where a young lad—Elie, aged nine and in fourth grade at the time—inspired me to write a success-oriented book for teens and young adults during one of my speaking appearances at the library To all the courageous teens and young adults who are making positive changes in their lives, daring to stand out to create the life of their dreams while working hard to make the world a better place To my late mother, Joy Ezinne (Good Mother) Obi, whom I listened to, obeyed, and respected while growing up and who shaped me by igniting the fire in me to become the person I am today. You enforced the principles of disciple, focus and gratitude in me which later became a moving force in my desire to succeed in the things I do. Mama, you were my greatest teacher and I miss, but still love you.

# FOREWORD

I write books, meaning I am an author—a published author. I also speak in public to empower people. That means I am a motivational speaker—one who brings out the best in others. I help people make positive changes to their lives. That's it. When I was young like you, I was very busy learning things that would make my life better. My mother gave birth to five children, and I was the third. That put me in the middle, a position I find very comfortable, because I am always protected from both the front and the back—two siblings on each side. Growing up in Nigeria, West Africa, my mother always told me to do the right things and taught me how to do them. I did very well in kindergarten, primary school, middle school, high school, and university because I listened to my parents. They taught me how to live a good life so that when I grew up, I would be fine. I did all they wanted me to do, and today I write books that help others live good lives. And that's why I wrote this book for you.

A lot of things helped me to become who I am today, and I will share these things with the hope that they will help you too. When I was a child, every morning when I woke up, I sang, prayed giving thanks for a new day. That was how we started each day. After that, I did my morning chores. Doing my morning chores made me feel happy and kept me in charge of my responsibilities. My mother made sure I completed them before getting ready for school. If I didn't do them, I will be spanked big time.

I went to school on time, because being late to school was a punishable offence. In school, I listened to my teachers. I kept away from the bad kids at the back of the class who made noise when the teacher was teaching. I asked challenging questions. That helped me develop a brain that is always asking questions and I learned a lot. My teachers liked me for that; they always wanted me around them and taught me new things. That's how I learned even more things. I had some challenges from my fellow students. My classmates called me "teacher's boy" and "bookworm," but it did not matter to me. I was never mad at them. They thought I read and knew a lot. I knew they were not smarter than me; they were just jealous. I kept away from them all the time.

In high school, I was good at soccer and played well, but I read my books every day and worked hard. I studied any book I could lay my hands on and listened to the news on the radio every day. My father had a small radio that we listened to at the time. We were close, and he taught me a lot. After I graduated secondary school, I went to university and did very well. Upon graduation, I was very lucky to get a resident visa to travel and live in America. I am very happy that I live in America today. I have written several books for adults, and I am grateful for America for giving me the opportunity to write. At some point, I decided to write this book to teach kids, teens, and young adults what I did to get to where I am now.

Now read on, have fun, practice what you read, and make your life better, starting now. Understand this: if you read this book but never practice what you read, it is useless. So you must practice until it becomes your second nature. Read and open your eyes to see the beauty of this book, written with love and inspiration to help you become a better person—someone whom your parents, community, and the world will be proud of in the near future. In this life, you have to find something that you like to do. That thing will be something that you like so much that you will want to do it anytime. That is called your "calling." Your calling is that thing you were created to do. If you pay attention to your calling now you are young and work it well, you will be happy in your life, and that can become your profession. That is what I did when I found out that my calling is in writing and public speaking. I took it and ran, and today, I am doing well. That is how life works. If you work hard at what you like to do, you will be happy to live your life to the fullest. Life will be good if you plan it well at a young age. How do you find and develop your calling? I will teach you now:

1. Get a pen and a piece of paper.
2. Keep calm for ten minutes, say nothing.
3. Write down three things you like to do.
4. Think about them carefully with your deepest concentration.
5. Delete one from the three, and think about the other two.
6. Pray for five minutes, and keep calm for ten minutes.
7. Now drop one more from the two.
8. The last thing remaining on the list is your calling.

Now, you can interpret your calling:

- If it has to do with math, then pay attention in math class.
- If it is related to singing, pay attention in music class.
- If it is related to animals, you should be seriously thinking about taking classes and leaning toward becoming a veterinarian.
- If you like journalism, you may be thinking of becoming a newscaster.

- If you like biology and cutting specimen animals in the lab, you may think of leaning toward becoming a surgeon.
- If it is related to sports, take it serious. Playing sports is good, but you can also be thinking of going to college for a degree so that if you are injured, you can fall back on your degree. Remember that contact sports are intense, and anything can happen. But this is not to frighten you—still be positive. This is how I developed my passion for writing and public speaking, and I am doing well at it.

I salute the American nation for giving me the opportunity to express my calling and to reach the world. You too can do the same if you work hard on your calling. I want to give you another piece of advice. You can have and develop two callings at the same time. So if one fails you in the future, you will fall back on the other. If two of them work well, then you will have two professions and two streams of income. You can do it, but you will have to work hard—really hard.  Hard work brings success. There are no shortcuts. It will not be easy at all, but you can achieve anything you want in this life as long as you work toward it without giving up, with determination and faith in yourself.  Every day is an opportunity for you to make the best of your life. Recognize the beautiful things around you. Help someone daily with joy and gratitude for the opportunity to help. You'll be happy every day if you do. Happiness brings good ideas to you so that you can create new things that will lead you to succeed.

Now make these declarations:

I am smart.
I am confident.
I am humble.
I am focused on my studies.
I am determined to succeed in life.

Finally, I charge you to do everything within your capacity to create a great life that will be a blessing to you, your family, your community and the world at large.

# ACKNOWLEDGMENTS

Writing a book takes time and energy. It is never one person's job; it is a team effort, a synergy of ideas from like minds. This means that a few people believed in this project and played their parts well in order for me to create this beautiful book. These are powerful people, and I want to salute them here for doing a great job.

Thank you to all my friends who believe in this movement for change and gratitude. Thank you to my project team who worked hard to get this book out to the world: Gaines Hill, my senior publishing consultant; Tara, Martha, Maria, Ray, my comprehensive copy editors at Amazon Group; Samuel Orellana- my book cover designer and everyone who purchased and read this book. We did it together.

# HOW TO USE THIS BOOK

I wrote this book to help teens and young adults make positive changes to their lives. If you read this book well, study it like a schoolbook, and do what is written here, you will learn many things that will change your life. I did these growing up to be where I am now. I am not selfish; so I decided to share these things with you in order to help you live a great life.

Before you start reading this book, get a dictionary, and keep it by your side. If you find a word you don't know, look it up, and use it to make a sentence. That's how to build your vocabulary. That is how I built mine, and today, I use words well, and people think I am smart. Actually, I am not intellectually gifted—I just read a lot. That's it. If you don't have a dictionary, ask your parents or family to buy one for you, or borrow one from the free public library in your community. After reading a chapter of this book, internalize it, and discuss what you read with your parents or friends. Then try to practice what you read. You can read every book on earth, but if you don't practice, it is of no use.

So read on, and enjoy the book. If you have questions or comments, I am more than happy to answer them. Simply e-mail me at azukazuke@gmail.com, and I will get right back to you.

Happy reading!

# A GOOD START

W hat does the word *good* mean? It means doing the right thing. In this chapter, I will teach you the things I did and how I did them. These were the good things I did that brought me to where I am today and will help you make the right decisions to start on a good note to live a good life. If you are living a good life already, I want you to make it better. A good start begins right at home. It starts right in your family—your father, mother, and other family members. Even if you live with only one of your parents, that's okay; no regrets, you can still have a good start in life. It is true that some children have bad experiences growing up. Some children have only one parent who really cared for them. But understand that even if no one cares for you, you can still live a great life.

Listening to your parents is good for you, because you will learn a lot from them. They came to life before you, so listen to them. My parents taught me so many good things because I listened. I got up in the morning and did my chores. Kids, always do your chores. Always do the things your parents tell you to do, as long as they're good things. When you are tired, tell them so that you can take a break. You have a right to take a break. But be polite. When you do that, they will love you more because you speak up with respect. A good start means you have to get up on time to get ready for school. Sleep early at night so that you will wake up strong. If you play video games all night, you will be tired, and you will wake up late. If you do something for twenty-one days, it becomes a habit that impacts your life for good.

Video games, computers, and TV are all good, but you have to be careful with them. They teach you good things, but can also kill your time. One thing I did growing up was always go to sleep early. My parents had a small black-and-white TV that we watched. But I went to bed on time after watching a few programs on so that I could wake up strong the next day. This helped me a lot. I always watch good things on TV, like good debates and world news. I have studied the lives of many successful people and found that they have one thing in common: they don't watch a lot of TV. TV can kill your dream of becoming successful in life. Stop watching too much TV, starting today. The library has lots of material for you to read. Go and read them. Form a habit of listening to world news and reading international newspapers, if you find them. That way you will know a lot about the world. Regardless of where you live today, you can still know where other countries are located on the map. That's a good geographical start for you in life. Knowledge is very power-ful, and no knowledge is a waste, so develop hunger for knowledge by reading a lot. Form a group of friends who will always empow-er you. Make friends with people who motivate you. Friends can make you happy or sad. Those who always make you sad should be cut off from your friendship, because they are up to no good. Stay around those who will teach you something useful. These friends are good to have. When I was your age, I carefully chose friends who were good people, respected people, obeyed people, worked hard, and had positive attitudes about life. That changed my mentality. My mother told me to always hang around them and avoid the bad ones. I did just that, and I am good today. So you have to choose your friends. The people around you determine how far you will go in life. Remember the popular sayings *"you are the average of the five people you hang around"* and *"tell me who your friends are, and I will tell you who you are."* You are not born to win or lose, but you can always choose what you want to be. The ball is in your court to play.

If you don't play, you let the ball pass you by. Never give up. If you continue to do the right things, study your books, stay focused, and reach out to people to ask mind developing questions, you will learn a lot. Your life will be shining so bright and will help you to choose your career. When choosing your career, it is important that you choose a career that gives you happiness. Choose a career that you love so much. Most adults today are unhappy because they chose the wrong careers. What happens? They are always angry on the job, unproductive, and they don't last on the job. I advise you to start thinking about what career to choose in life today. I chose writing because I like to write, and I write well. I also like to help people change their lives for good. I am happy doing what I do and will do it as long as I live. Change the way you think. Start thinking about the positive things that will make your future better. Your thinking affects your life. If you think you will have a good career, you will, but you must work hard. If you think you will fail in school, then you will likely fail in school. So always think positive thoughts.

If you think your parents are tough on you, then most likely, they will be. If you think and strongly believe that you can achieve anything you want, then you can. But you have to work hard to make that happen. If you don't work hard, your dreams will crash. President Barack Obama believed he could be the president of the United States, and he did just that. But he did not sit at home gossiping, being lazy, watching television, and playing video games all night. He stepped out, working hard in school, in college, and in the community, He built his career and made it happen.

To achieve something great in your life, you must be organized. This means you must be neat in your appearance; early to school, meetings, and class events; and well cultured. When you are organized, many good people will like you and will want you around them. These people will teach you new things, and you can also share ideas. Try to learn something new every day. This could be just a new word in the dictionary. Learn one new word every day from the dictionary. That will improve your knowledge of vocabulary. When you come across any word you don't know in this book, look it up in your dictionary to learn the meaning. Before I close this chapter, I want to salute you for taking the courage to read this book up to this page. It is not easy to form the habit of reading, but if you do, in the long run, you will be blessed. Reading changes you, so keep on reading. Now I want you to make the following declarations. Read it with passion and with all your heart. Come back to this page often, and read these declarations until they master your thinking. They will change your life with time for the better.

- I am born to do great things.
- I am doing great things, and I am just starting.
- I will finish high school, and I will go to college.
- I will finish college because I know college is important.
- I also know education is very important in my life.
- Nelson Mandela said that *education is the key to life*, and I believe it.
- I will give it my all and do my best in school.
- I complete my homework all the time.
- I am calm and cool, and I work hard every day improving my life.
- I think of the great future I want for myself every day.
- I have the support of my family, friends, teachers, and community.
- I will make a good life. I know it, I believe it, and I am working toward it.

Now raise your right hand in the air and congratulate yourself in advance. You have to do that often, even when no one congratulates you. That's a great secret to developing power and good energy to create big things.

## Success Story

Motivational speaker and author Les Brown never knew his parents. He grew up under his adopted mother. But he always read books, did the right thing, and had strong faith. Today Les Brown is a great speaker, and he travels the world teaching people how to live a good life. So learn from his story, and keep doing good. You will be fine.

## Exercise for Building Success

Describe the type of relationship you have with your parents, family, and close friends in eight sentences. How do you intend to improve these relationships?

1.
2.
3.
4.
5.
6.
7.
8.

# LISTEN TO YOUR PARENTS
# AND SENIORS

Your parents are the closest people to you. They are always around you. If you have only one parent taking care of you, that's okay. You can still live a good life. You can still be anything you want to be. One thing that helped me while I was growing up was that I listened to my parents all the time. I obeyed them and did the right thing. When I made a mistake, they corrected me. When I did something bad, it had consequences. It did not happen often, because I tried to do the right thing. This helped shape my life to be a good person. So listen to your parents, take their advice, and do the right thing. If your parents tell you to do something that makes you sad, do not stay in the corner of the room crying; get yourself together, and talk to them in a private area to express how you feel about what happened. That shows respect and humility. Even if your parents are not living together, still listen to your dad or mom. Find someone you can rely on, and adopt that person as your mother or father by choice. If you respect this person, he or she will pour his or her heart out to support you and play a parental role in your life. If you step up to make that plea, you will be accepted as one of his or her own. Do not keep things that worry you to yourself. Tell someone, talk to your teacher, talk to a good friend, or talk to a neighbor for help. If you seek help, you will always find it.

Another good thing to do is pray together with your family. Prayers changes things. I know this. Prayers mean asking with humility for what you want in your life. Don't pray for yourself alone; pray for others as well. Pray for the state, the country, and the nation. When you form the habit of praying, your eyes will be opened to the right things, and you will not have any time for garbage or feeding your mind with nonsense. Parents came to the world before you, so they have many experiences. Listening to them will change your life in amazing ways. When parents advise you about the friends you have, please pay attention.

Be nice to your parents. When they correct you, do not be angry; rather, remember that they are there to guide you and assist you become a better person. Respect your parents, and listen to their opinions and viewpoints. Even when they get you angry, respect them, and keep calm. It is all for your good. But speak up when you have to. You have a right to speak up too. Your parents and teachers correct you because they want you to succeed in life. They don't hate you. They love you and want the best for you, so pay attention. Learning how to respect them now teaches you how to respect other people in the future, especially random people you meet on your various paths in life. What type of friends do you keep? Who are your friends? Are they hardworking? Are they doing their homework? Do they curse, gossip, or hang around the streets with their pants on their knees? If these types of people are your friends, you are in the wrong group. It is time to move away from them and run for your future. If you continue to hang around them, you will be miserable. You'll be worth nothing in the future, and you may not even graduate high school or college. Stay away from those who curse, tell lies, or disrespect people. You will never learn anything from them. Make friends with those who tell the truth and respect people. Hang around those who are serious about school and education. When your parents send you to school, you'd better go to school, because it will pay off later. I did one thing that changed my life when I was in school: I always sat in the front row. When you go anywhere, sit in front. It shows that you are serious to learn. Leaders like people who sit in front, and they connect better with them and will want to help them grow better in what they do. Teachers are leaders, pastors are leaders, and motivational speakers are leaders. Leaders are everywhere. Teachers lead you to greatness, but you must listen. Teachers are like angels who teach you things that make you a better person. Don't take them for granted. Respect them. Every new day you spend with your parents is an opportunity to learn something from them. Never take their presence for granted, for one day you may not see them anymore. Take advantage of their presence in your life. Take advantage of the people in your life today, and listen to them as they speak. You learn more by listening than talking.

When people are talking, listen until they finish. Then you can say something. Don't wait to reply right away to show that you know something. You may miss important information by talking too much. Learn every day and fight hard to become the person you want to be. No one will do that but you. You can get help from people, but most of the work will be done by you. You will be fine as long as you are doing something good every day. It will not happen overnight. Don't be in a rush to succeed. Remember the baby went though many stages before becoming an adult. It takes time. Slowly, gradually, and with patience, you will make progress. Avoid people who never teach you anything good. They are useless in your life. Learn a lot from people who want to see you succeed. Life is about knowing more, changing, and making the best out of every day. You don't know what will happen next. So learning and changing is good for you.

Are you a bully? Are you bullying others? Bullying is very disrespectful. It's a bad practice. It's morally wrong, and it's a very dangerous game. Don't be caught up in that nonsense. When you bully others, you are telling them that you are disrespectful, you are not focused, and you live a low life. Bullying comes in different forms—name-calling, making funny gestures, pushing others, laughing sarcastically, hair pulling, beating, and many other forms. When you bully others, you are being useless, and let me tell you something here: most students who bully others end up in trouble. Most of them do not graduate, because they focus on the wrong things, fail their classes, and as such, can't qualify for college. Most bullies end up doing drugs on the streets. You do not want to be there.

So do the right thing in school: avoid bullying others, and make your parents and your school proud. When you are bullied, do not bully back; rather, reach out to someone to make a complaint. Reach out to your teachers, your counselors in school, or your parents. You must talk to someone about it right away. Do not keep it to yourself, because if you do, and it continues, it will be so much that someday, you may not be able to bear it anymore and will vent the anger out. That can put you in trouble too. So the best thing to do is to report it right away and let someone look into it.

One thing I teach in my speaking classes is the importance of admitting mistakes. When you make a mistake, own up to it, admit it, and apologize right away. Even if you are wrong, sometimes it is better to apologize and move on to more important things.

There are many people out there to distract you from focus. They know it, and they come right to put you off track. Why should you allow that to happen? Your time is too precious to be wasted on rubbish.

You have to be content with what you have. Never compare yourself with others. That is a very dangerous act. Always appreciate people. Do not take anyone for granted—not even the homeless man on the street. Understand that you too could be homeless, so do not make fun of anyone you meet, even if they don't look like you. You are not better that anyone, and no one is better than you either. No matter your color, your height, their color, their height, your size, their size or where they come from, everyone deserves respect. When you respect others, they respect you too. So do not talk down or make jokes about people, especially people you don't know. You have no idea where you will meet them in the future, so be wise, and respect everyone you meet.

Accept change. Life is about change. Things happen all the time. No matter what happens in your life and in your family, accept the change in good faith. Good or bad, accept the change, get used to it, make the adjustments needed, and move on.

Use your talents well. Focus on using the gifts that you have to create a great life that your parents will be proud of. If you know how to sing, sing like you are a champion. If you know how to dance, keep dancing. If your talent is in motivational speaking, you better start speaking. If you like to make jokes, keep making jokes—but only good jokes. You never know if you will be the next Chris Rock or Kevin Hart. Keep being you, and keep doing what you like to do as long as it is something positive that can change your life for better. Develop a habit of not only spending more listening time with your parents but also with everyone who cares to honestly speak to you. Listen more, and talk less; that way, you'll learn more from people. A listening ear is a learning ear.

### Success Story

I am a success story today in my own little way, because I listened to my teachers while in school. I did all my homework and went to school on time and did well in class. I always sat in front. I was very happy with myself and always looked for ways to do better. While in high school, I respected my teachers, did my homework on time, and worked very hard. I was always on time and rarely missed school. This helped shape me into a good person, and today, I am a product of the seeds I sowed into my life. I am a published author of four books on amazon.com and a motivational speaker, and I travel the world, motivating people to live their dreams.

### A QUOTE TO INSPIRE YOU

*"We will either find a way, or make one."*

-HANNIBAL

## Exercise for Building Success

Write down eight bad habits that you have. Write how you will change each habit.

1.
2.
3.
4.
5.
6.
7.
8.

# WORK VERY HARD

The person who works hard always wins. Hard work means doing the right thing every single day with determination. When you work hard in school by doing your homework and studying hard, you will come out with good grades. Hard work makes good grades. Read your books when you get home from school or on holidays. Stay the course.

Visit the library when you are free at least three times a week in order to read other books not related to your studies. That way, you will learn new things. The library is a free resource center. Libraries will change your life. The more you read, the more you'll know. Hard work is a tough game. It involves making sacrifices by doing hard things now that will change your life later. Read newspapers too. The library has lots of them. Visit the library to work hard by doing things that will change your life later. If you read every day for twenty-one days, it will become your habit, and you will never stop reading. It is okay to watch television, but don't do it all day. There are many programs on television you don't need. Most of them are distractions that do you no good. When I was a teenager, I not only studied things within the curriculum of my grade but I also worked extra by studying subjects that were way above my class standards. I learned so much doing this. It really opened my mind to the possibilities of what I could achieve by working hard.

Hard work pays off. It helps build your character. When you are working hard to complete a task, your entire mind is focused on that task, and that has a way of improving the way you see things. The greatest advantage of hard work is that it gets results. When you work hard, you get results. And when you get results, you will be happy. Hard work makes people recognize and respect you. So when you are doing something, know that someone is watching. Your hard work will make people want to know and like you. But if you are a lazy student, no one will want to be around you. People like to be with those who achieve things. When people like you, they will support you and will always be there when you need them. Hard work also opens doors of good things for you. To do well in life, you have to put in your best in all you do, including working hard in school and at home. Your work, your future, and your belief in yourself must be ahead of everything. Do the things that bring honor to you and your family. Decide what you want to do in your life, and go for it. But remember to get rest too. Rest is very important to make your body stronger for hard work. Exercising also helps with hard work, because it reduces stress. Do small things that make you happy. That way, you'll feel good doing the big things. Choose big thing you want to achieve in life. I will teach you how to work on toward success.

- Break down how you want to achieve it into small steps.
- Do something every day to work toward it, like studying about it.
- Talk to trusted people to advise you on how to proceed.

- Go to the library to research more about how to go about it.
- Start doing it right now, and never give up.
- Celebrate once you achieve it, and move to the next bigger project.

There are twenty-four hours in a day, and they're all yours to use the way you want. You either use it well, or you waste it all. You can decide to spend all your time playing video games, wasting your life, or you can use your time well to study.

I am not saying that video games are bad, but you do not want to play them all the time. That wastes your time for creativity. One big secret to success is time management. Time is precious. Stop anything that is distracting you from your studies. Stop making friends with negative people so that you can focus on success. If what you are doing is not making you get closer to success, then stop it right away.

Every day, do something that you will be proud of. You can read a page of this great book, exercise for twenty minutes, help someone in need, or run errands for your parents. Just do something that will make you happy. Keep learning every day. Your best days are not behind you. They are right in front of you, so focus your attention on your future, where you will live the rest of your life.

Never give up. Do not think that life will always be easy. Life is never easy; it is tough, but you can succeed. It will be tough, easy, and tough again, and it may even get tougher, but if you stay positive and keep working toward your dream, you will make it in life. Sometimes you will meet great challenges, hard times, and failures, but do not stop working hard. You will be fine if you hang in there. Never give up.

Stay close to people who push you forward. Surround yourself with peers who are also doing good things in school and in your community. That way, you will stay motivated and inspired. If you hang around successful people, you will want to be successful too.

Every time you achieve one small thing, celebrate, and move on to the next big one. Do not stop improving yourself. With time, your life will be so good that others will want to copy you as a role model for excellence. Won't you feel good about that?

When I was growing up in West Africa, my late mother always taught me the importance of hard work. She told me that if I worked hard and stayed focused, I would achieve a lot, but if I did not work hard and spent all night watching television, I would achieve nothing. I took her advice to heart and never looked back.

### Success Stories

Barak Obama, the first black president of the United States succeeded because he worked hard in high school, in college, and even after college. He was raised by a single mother because his father had died when he was very young. But it never stopped him from becoming a success story. I like his swag, and I respect him a lot.

Ben Carson had a long hardship growing up in Detroit. His mom never went to school. His dad left the family. His schoolmates thought he knew nothing. But these things did not stop him. He worked very hard to become a brain doctor—a neurosurgeon. You can do the same or even better than Ben.

## A QUOTE TO INSPIRE

*"It is not enough to have a good mind; the main thing is to use it well."*

*-RENE DESCARTES*

**Exercise for Building Success**

Write down eight big goals you want to achieve in your life before you reach the age of thirty. Write down one major step you will take to achieve each goal. You can put these eight goals on your vision board as your dream builder.

1.
2.
3.
4.
5.
6.
7.
8.

# SHARPEN YOUR MORAL VALUES

I have published a few books for adults on Amazon.com to share some of the things that changed my life and brought me to where I am today. A major factor that has contributed to my success so far is the belief in the moral values that my parents taught me while I was growing up in Africa. I will share them with you. If you start practicing these things now while you are young, over time, it will become your second nature, and you will be on the road to an exciting life. I will discuss these values in bullet format to break it down for you.

- Learn to forgive others. When people do bad things to you, it hurts, but carrying the emotions in your heart without letting go is not good for your health. Whenever you nurse the feeling of revenge or anger over someone who hurt you, your blood pressure and heart rate rises. This is bad for you. Secondly, carrying the emotions slows down your progress. Most times, the person who hurt you has moved on and is busy enjoying life while you are busy getting angry. Forgive people easily. It benefits your health.

- Respect others. Make it a habit. Respecting people means you value them. When you respect people, they respect you too, and they will like you and support you when you need help. Someone you respect will be willing to give you a recommendation when you need it or a referral that will help you later in life. It will even help you with college admissions. Never talk down on others.

- Be there for people. Be available when they need help. That does not mean that you will give all your time assisting others. But when you can, do it with happiness. As you show people that you are there for them, they will be there for you when you need them. They will also remember you when there is something good to give away. This is because the first person that will come to their mind will be you because you are there for them too.

- Have self-control. One major thing that puts teens and young adults in trouble is lack of self-control. When someone makes you angry, ask yourself, is this worth getting upset about? Then take a deep breath, and walk away. If it continues, try to talk to the person about it, and talk to someone to address it. If you don't control yourself when upset, you may do something really bad and put yourself in a big trouble.

- Be humble. When you're humble, people will like you and will want to work with you. Humility means respecting people and not being bigheaded. People who are humble always get ahead in life, because people like them and support them. So be humble. Humility makes people respect you and want to support you. Humility has helped me a lot in my life, and I am still benefiting from it. So be humble; it paves way for success.

- Do not gossip. Gossiping means talking behind someone's back. It is a very bad thing. People do not like to be around those who gossip. If you gossip, you will gradually lose all of your friends. Also, you can get yourself in trouble by gossiping. When people know you as someone who does not gossip, they will open up and share useful information with you.

- Never destroy property. Property damage include breaking chairs, pulling grass from the field, throwing things at windows, or painting walls with graffiti. Property damage is very bad and can ruin your reputation. You can get in trouble too. You can also hurt yourself in the process. It may ruin your record, which may affect you in a bad way in the future. So stay away from destroying property at home, at school, and anywhere at all.

- Be patient. Life can be tough sometimes. The teen years are a trying period, and most people lose their patience around this time. Do not be one of them. Patience means waiting until it's the right time. You can't change things you can't control, so be patient. When things don't go the way you want right away, be patient. If you are not patient, you can do the wrong thing and make things worse.

- Volunteer often. Volunteerism helps a lot in life. It means giving some of your free time to the others. Volunteering has many benefits. You will be recognized in your community as a giver and make new friends by meeting other volunteers. You will earn credits for high school or college. It helps you in the future when you start looking for a job. It makes you happy. It is good for your health. Always find ways to give back by volunteering.

- Be courageous. Never let anyone tell you that you can't achieve anything. Courage makes you feel strong with belief that you can achieve anything you set your mind to. If you stay strong now, while you are young, you will carry it to adulthood, and you will be a strong person.

- Obey street rules. Always walk on the sidewalks. If there are no sidewalks, walk in the areas designated for pedestrians. Don't disobey the law by creating your own laws. The society is an orderly place, so you must be orderly in your behaviors. Obey the street signs. If you don't, you may get into an accident, and that can delay your goals, or you may even die. You don't want to die young, do you? Do not hang out on the major roads. They're for cars. Obey the rules, and preserve your life.
- Respect the law and the police. The law respects you if you respect the law. Police officers are your friends, and they will respect you if you respect them. Whenever you are approached by the cops, stay calm, and listen to them. Do not answer any question not asked. Answer what they ask you, and be brief. Do not challenge them. Do not argue, try to hurt, or insult them. Don't be angry when they talk to you. Be polite to them, and smile. The cops like to smile too; they are humans. It's the nature of their job that makes them look serious all the time. Remember that a lot of teens and young adults have lost their lives due to their recklessness with the cops. You don't want to be in the statistics. If you do something wrong and are approached by the cops, tell the truth, apologize, and feel sorry for your actions. They are human too, will work with you, correct you and can even give you a second chance.
- When stopped by the cops, what you say is very important. Anything you say can be used against you and can give them reason to arrest you, especially if you bad-mouth or hit a police officer.
- Show cops any documents or ID they request, whether you are driving, a passenger, or just walking down the

street. Cops are there to protect you, so don't be scared of their presence. If you do the right thing, why be scared of them?

- Do not give them wrong name. They've got the skills to find out, so be honest.
- Do not try to disrupt their job; they can arrest you.
- Think before you say anything. You have a brain, use it wisely.
- Don't make a bad movement or suspicious body language, and don't yell at them. Rather, keep calm, and smile to show them that you are not nervous and that you are willing to cooperate with them.
- Do not get into any argument with the police. Cops don't have time for that rubbish.
- Keep your hands where they can see them.
- Never try to run, even if you did something wrong.
- Do not try to touch any police officer or try to be friendly. Be professional.
- Do not resist at all. Even if you're right, just keep calm. The cops will eventually let you go, and you can move on with your life intact.

**Success Story**

I grew up under my parents. They made sure I had all I needed as a child, especially the things that had to do with my basic education. My parents taught me many moral values that have guided me to become the person I am today. I am an author and motivational speaker with a university education. I am living a life of inspiration, empowering the world to live their dreams. You can learn a few things from my book. I don't know everything, but I know how to help people make positive changes in their lives.

## A QUOTE TO INSPIRE YOU

*I learned that the only way you are going to get anywhere in life is to work hard at it. Whether you're a musician, a writer, an athlete, or a businessman, there is no getting around it. If you do, you'll win, if you don't, you won't.*

-BRUCE JENNER
Olympic gold medalist- decathlon

**Exercise for Building Success**

Write down eight moral values that you need to work on to improve your life. Write down one thing you have to do right away (starting today) to improve each of these values.

1.

2.

3.

4.

5.

6.

7.

8.

# GET DAILY EXERCISE

Exercise is very good for you. Exercise benefits your body in many ways. Walking is one the most common exercises that you can do. It's free and can be done anywhere, such as at the park, in the backyard, at the mall, in the field, and at school.

Exercise promotes good health. Walking is a form of exercise that requires no equipment. When you exercise, you feel healthy and strong. A healthy body gives you the strength to work hard in life. Exercise keeps your weight in a healthy range. Obesity is now a worldwide epidemic. The major cause is lack of exercise. People wait until they weigh so much, before starting to exercise. You don't want to do that. Exercise should be a daily program and a regular part of life. A lot of young adults today are overweight because of a lack of exercise and because of the types of food they eat. Try to eat a lot of vegetables and fruits to reduce your weight. Go easy on white bread and soda (soft drinks).

Soda is bad for you. It has lots of sugar. This sugar goes into your body and stays there. Some sugar is flushed out of your body, but a lot of it stays there and can make you put on weight or even develop diabetes. So stop drinking soda if you can, and drink more water. Water cleanses your body and is the best drink. One other thing I would like to discuss here is smoking. If you don't smoke, do not attempt it. Do not give adults money to buy you cigarettes if you are underage. Smoking cigarettes kills your body and can cause lung cancer. Even when you become an adult, do not smoke. It is bad for your health.

Adding exercise into your life has benefits. Make sure it is okay with your doctor before you start. Walk up the stairs instead of taking the elevator whenever you can. Do twenty push-ups a day. Join other students when they go out for exercise. It is more fun doing it together. Take your dog for a walk in the evening. Do twenty sit-ups at home every morning. Kids are now developing belly fat, and that is concerning. Sit-ups reduce belly fat. Do not watch too much TV. Even if you are watching your favorite program, do five few push-ups during commercial breaks. Exercise makes you feel good and keeps you alert. Those who are active when they're young are active when they get older. Exercise strengthens your body, and makes your brain sharp to retain information. You will learn better in school when you exercise daily. Exercise gives you more strength to do your chores and schoolwork.

I like to write about eating good foods in my books. We were taught in school to eat foods that have carbohydrates, good fats and oils, fiber, and protein. Good food is very important for health. If you don't eat good food, you may not think well. A body deprived of good food does not function well. Good foods are vegetables, whole foods, fruits, and nuts, like peanuts, walnuts, and cashews. You can help your parents when they shop by telling them to buy healthy foods. They are not too costly. A few extra dollars will get you the good foods instead of the junk foods. Hamburgers are not good for you. Ask your parents to cook at home more often. They will save more money if they make healthy food at home.

Drink at least six to eight glasses of water daily. It makes you feel good and keeps you hydrated. Don't wait until you are tasty to drink water; just drink it throughout the day. It is good for you. Your body needs water to work well. Water is of major importance to the body. The human body is made up of about 60 percent water. So you see that you really need lots of water for your body to function well. You can create a plan to drink water at the top of every hour. For example, you can drink a small glass of water at seven, eight, nine, and ten o'clock, or you can drink every two hours at eight, ten, twelve, two, and four o'clock. Make it a point of duty to drink a minimum of eight glasses of water daily.

Water plays these roles in the body:

- Regulates body temperature. That's why your body is hot if you don't drink water.
- Acts to absorb shock in the brain. For example, if your head is shaken, water helps support the brain to avoid injury.
- Helps in the digestion of food.
- Helps to transport oxygen to all parts of the body.
- Helps to keep joints moist so that you aren't injured when you exercise.
- Flushes waste products from the body. When you urinate, water helps flush out the bad metabolites from your body.
- Water helps make the saliva in our mouth needed for proper digestion of food. Digestion of food starts in the mouth—that's Biology 101.

Fruits are good for you. Many fruits contain vitamin C, which helps heal wounds and fight diseases. Apples are good fruits. They lower the levels of the bad cholesterol and improve the good cholesterol. Oranges and grapes have lots of vitamin C. The right amount of fruits and vegetables taken in on a daily basis is good for your body. But it might be very difficult to get the right amount of vegetables and fruits in on a daily basis. To do this, you can blend different fruits together into a smoothie, and drink it. You can do this with a vegetable smoothie too. I do that a lot, especially in the mornings. With the adequate amount of vitamins in your body, you are stronger and healthier.

We live in a society where we have so much food, but people are malnourished. This is because a lot of people are used to eating high-calorie foods that taste good instead of low-calorie foods that don't taste as good. The high-calorie foods make you put on weight, because they are filled with sugars that are not good for the body. Encourage your family to add lots of vegetables to the weekly food menu, because they are good for health. Vegetables and fruits have lots of vitamins, which are good for proper body functioning. When you eat lots of vegetables, you have lots of vitamins in your body. This helps to fight diseases.

Vitamins are good for proper body functioning. (Remember, if you do not understand the meaning of any word in this book, you know what to do: look it up in your dictionary! That's how to build your knowledge of words. And you never know when you will develop love for Scrabble—you could even become the next world Scrabble champion!) There are many types of vegetables you can eat. You can work with your family to buy them from the store. Spinach, cauliflower, broccoli, lettuce, and carrots are the common ones you know. These are also many other amazing vegetables at the supermarket that you can add to your menu. Vegetables help you maintain a healthy weight.

In our world today, teens and young adults are becoming overweight. That is not good. For example, it is not good when a ten-year-old kid weighs 150 pounds. That is a huge stress on the heart, which pumps blood to all parts of the body. This can even cause diabetes. To keep your weight in check, you have to watch what you eat. The more junk food you eat, the more you risk becoming overweight. Eating healthy food and having a normal weight is better than eating junk now and paying later by being overweight. Think about that.

Do something every day to challenge your body. Exercise keeps you strong and sharpens your brain to learn better in school. It helped me a lot when I was young, and it continues to help me now. So develop a habit of exercising weekly. You can start by exercising once a week for thirty minutes in the comfort of your home or backyard, or you can go to the park, where you may meet your peers to form an exercise group to make it even more fun.

### Success Story

Serena Williams plays tennis. That is a form of exercise. But she turned it into a huge profession and is today making millions of dollars playing a sport that is the form of exercise that she likes most. Her sister, Venus, is doing the same thing, and they are very happy and successful. So you see, a form of exercise can be a way for you to make a good living in your life. Serena may have started playing tennis as a hobby, but it turned into a money-making profession. Think about it. If you like to run, do it well. If you like to play basketball, do it well. If you like to play soccer or another form of exercise—you got it, do it.

## A QUOTE TO INSPIRE YOU

*You have to believe in yourself when no one else does.*
*That's what makes you a winner.*

## - VENUS WILLIAMS
Olympic gold medalist and professional tennis player

## Exercise for Building Success

Write down eight types of exercise that you can do that I did not discuss in this chapter. You can do research on them. That's another way to learn.

1.
2.
3.
4.
5.
6.
7.
8.

# BE NICE TO PEOPLE—VOLUNTEER

One easy way to work toward success is by being humble and respectful. Humility attracts attention. Always respect and be nice to people. When you respect people, you will be respected too. Also, people will like you and support you when you need their help. People will not like you if you disrespect them. When you meet people, smile and shake their hands with firmness, and say, "*I am happy to meet you.*" If you start to do this at this young age, it will become part of you, and you will build confidence and gain the respect of others. Also try to remember people's names. Call people by their first names when you meet them again. That's a way of saying "you're important, and I remember your name." Be nice to everyone, including strangers, but do not trust strangers until you get to know them. When you are nice to people, they will be nice to you and teach you things when you ask.

Form the habit of helping out whenever you can. It is called giving. Help out in your community when you can. Volunteer your time and energy. When you volunteer your time, you can get extra credit for high school or college. It will be in your records that you give back. You can also volunteer in your local church. There are so many things to do to help in your community. Research these things. That's how to learn. Your community cannot do it all. You can volunteer to assist in some way. You will learn the power of giving as you volunteer, feel good and you will be blessed in return.

You can help by serving coffee after service in your church—that's volunteering or help out cleaning up afterward. Remember that whatever you give to people (be it in service or otherwise) will come back to you in the measures in which you give. You give to receive. Part of my success today is because I give all the time. I give help, I give money, I give inspiration, I give hope, I give positive energy, I smile a lot, and I give smiles to people all the time. I also like taking selfies, and as a selfie author, I use the power of selfies to bring out smiles in people's faces. That is giving too. But you don't have to give the things that I give. Just find what you can give without hurting, and give it. But you must give with happiness in order to receive the rewards. So give and move on.

Visit community events, and find somewhere to volunteer your time. The best place to volunteer your time is in your community. When you do, people will recognize you, and they will like to do more things with you. Volunteering will also help you when you start searching for a job in the future. Remember that this is the time to start building your résumé for the future. The seeds you sow into your life today are the fruits you'll reap in the future. Your future is not too far from now, so this is the time to start doing things to invest in your future. A part of this involves building your résumé by volunteering. Think about it this way: it takes the same amount of time to hang out with bad kids on the streets as it does to volunteer in your community. The difference is that hanging out on the streets will never bring you anything good. But volunteering will bring you a good name and expose you to people you may never have met. These people will likely help you in the future, including giving you a good reference when you are ready for college.

There are many opportunities for volunteering. You can volunteer at your school. You don't need too many hours to volunteer. All you need are a few hours a week to show that you have a giving heart and want to give back to your community. When you form the habit of giving, you will always receive things in return. Remember the saying *"It is more blessed to give than to receive."* Giving opens doors for big things to come into your life. Volunteering is a form of giving, so when you volunteer, you are giving. You can even volunteer in your family. You can volunteer to set the dinner table every evening at home. That's giving back to your family. It does not take anything away from you to do it. Even the habit of making money works like that too. If you make money for twenty-one days, you will get excited about it and will want to continue making more and more. That's how it works with volunteering too.

This is the time to start investing in your future. Your future is very important, and this is where you will spend the rest of your life. So start investing in your future now. Take it very seriously. It does not matter if you have just learned that today or not. There are so many opportunities out there for growth. Take advantage of them now that you are young.

Today is a great day to start as long as you take it very seriously. I am still investing in my future, and this is something I started when I was younger. I am still a work in progress. Giving back and volunteering have changed my life and turned me into a giving machine. I did not start giving overnight. It is something I did for years, starting when I was very young like you. Giving makes you feel good as long as you give with joy.

I want to share a story with you. I was coming out of the gym one day, and I saw this homeless guy walking toward me, looking sad, bruised, and dirty. As I saw him approaching me, I walked toward him and shook his hand. That put a smile on his face right away. He told me how he was homeless and had been beaten and burned by a group of bad boys. His hands had first-degree burns, and according to him, he had just been treated and released from the hospital. I took pity on him, told him that he would be okay, and gave him a hug with a comforting pat on the upper back. He felt even better and opened up to tell me that he had not eaten since the last night and was very hungry. I told him that he is in good hands, would make sure he will eat some good meal and told him I will drive to go get him food. Apparently, he didn't believe me at first, because when I came back, he said, "I didn't think you would come back, because people lie a lot." We sat next to a concrete wall on the outside of the gym, and he ate and drank his water as we talked. He learned that I am originally from Nigeria, West Africa. That blew his mind and got him even more excited. He told me that he guessed so from my accent. He said that he had received numerous gifts and help from Nigerians in the past, so he could pick up our accent. He said, "It seems they like to give a lot to those who don't have." I was humbled. After he ate, we took a selfie for remembrance, and he asked that I share it, hoping he could get more help. You see, you never know whom will appear on your path to be blessed. I felt so good after that. I went into my car and left while praying for the next opportunity to give. You don't have to give like me, because you may not have the money, but you can give something. You can tell someone who is not feeling well to get better soon. You can send a text to someone taking a test and wish them well. You can help senior citizens run an errand. You can babysit a neighbor's child while your neighbor runs out to the store to pick up a few groceries. There are many ways you can be of help to the world of which you are a part, and it will come back to bless you in return and help you grow morally into a good and successful person.

**Success Story**
President Barack Obama started out volunteering a lot in his community while growing up. Later, he started doing community organizing, and from there, he became very famous in America. Then when he ran for presidency, he was voted as the first black president of the United Sates.

## A QUOTE TO INSPIRE YOU

*"Nine-nine percent of all failures come from people who have a habit of making excuses."*

### -GEORGE WASHINGTON CARVER

## Exercise for Building Success
What do you understand by the term volunteering?


Write down eight different ways you can volunteer in your community this year.

1.
2.
3.
4.
5.
6.
7.
8.

# BE THANKFUL EVERY DAY

I write adult success and motivational books. One of the topics I always discuss in my books is gratitude. Gratitude means being thankful. I love to discuss gratitude in my books, because it changed my life. My life may not be what it is today if not for the power of gratitude. Every day is New Year's Day for me, and I celebrate it with gratitude. Gratitude means being thankful for the things you have now, the things you had yesterday, the things you will have tomorrow, and everything happening in your life. People who are always thankful are always happy. Do you know why? Because they see beauty and happiness in the little things that most people don't see. They see joy in things like trees, schoolchildren walking to school, the smell of coffee in the kitchen, the songs on radio, the clean water flowing from the tap, the moon, their hands, their ability to see, or their wheelchairs or canes for mobility if they are physically challenged.

What are you grateful for today? That's a question I want you to answer.

- Be thankful for your parents who brought you to this world.
- Be grateful for your eyes, your nose, your ears, and your mouth.
- Be grateful for your mother. Even if she is not there for you, still be grateful.
- Be grateful for your father. Even if he is not involved, it's okay to be grateful.
- Be thankful for your teachers.
- Be thankful for your good friends.
- Be thankful for the security guard in your school who keep you safe.
- Be grateful for the water you drink.
- Be grateful for the person who cleans the community streets you take on your way to school. When you see this person next time, stop and say, "Thank you for the work you do." It will make that person happy. That's gratitude.
- Be grateful for the older lady who serves food in the school kitchen and the little man who serves soup. Tell them how good they are in what they do. They will feel good and bless you.

One day I was travelling to speak at an event and needed to put gas in my car. I stopped at a gas station, and this man in his late sixties pumped gas into my car. As I was leaving, I gave him a one-dollar bill and said, "Please, just take this little tip." He said that it was a lot of money for him. That blew my mind. So I gave him five extra dollars. He was so touched that he could not say a word. He just touched my head and said, "God bless you." Then he walked away. That made my day. But you don't have to give money if you do not have it. You can always just say, "Thank you so much," and mean it. What you give comes right back to you.

- When you wake up in the morning, be thankful for the new day. It's a blessing. Do you think you are special to be alive? No, but it's a blessing, so be thankful. Read your books, help out, or serve. Just do something that you'll be proud of every day.

- Be thankful for what you have now, no matter how small, and don't compare yourself with others. If your parents cannot buy you those costly Michael Jordan sneakers, please don't be mad at them. Be grateful for the used ones you have. At the right time, you will have the brand names. Don't be greedy; be patient, but work and hope for better days.

- Never underrate others who do not have as much as you do. Be happy for them, respect them, but don't make fun of them. Wish your friends blessings and pray for them so that they too can have.

- Do not be too bigheaded for anything you have now. That is called pride. It is not good. Remember, "pride goes before a fall." Be grateful for your hands, your legs to walk, your ears to hear, and your brain to think.

- Be thankful for the food you eat. Never take it for granted. Food keeps you alive.

- If you walk to school, be grateful that you have legs. Some people don't have legs. They use prosthetic legs, yet are very happy and they work hard doing big things.

- Be grateful for your clothes, shoes, and everything else you wear on your body. They're all blessings. If you don't have brand names but want them, be grateful and patient, and at the right time, you will have them.

- Be grateful for the trees lining the streets. They produce oxygen that we breathe and that keeps us alive.

**Success Story**

I am a living example of someone whose life has been transformed by the power of gratitude. I grew up having little under the guidance of my parents. Mum was always there for me. Dad was not as much due to his schedules. Mum taught me the power of gratitude even when things seemed tough. It became part of me, and I still practice gratitude to this day. As a child, I always gave thanks for anything that happened in my life, whether good or bad. I even gave thanks for everything in advance. I gave thanks for living and working in America in advance. But it paid off, because over time, I had the opportunity to immigrate to and work in the United States. I am doing well today, writing books and empowering people as a motivational speaker. That is how gratitude changed my life. It can change yours too.

## A QUOTE TO INSPIRE YOU

*"Change is the law of life. And those who look only to the past or present are certain to miss the future.*

- JOHN F. KENNEDY
Thirty-fifth president of the United States.

## Exercise for Building Success

Write down eight things you are most grateful for this year. Write down why you are grateful for each one. Does that make you happy?

1.
2.
3.
4.
5.
6.
7.
8.

# YOU CAN BE ANYTHING YOU WANT

I want you to say this ten times and mean it: "I can be anything I want to be." Write it on a white piece of paper, and place it where you will see it every morning. Read it aloud once you wake up and before you sleep at night. I call this "calling things into your life." It changed my life, and I know it will change yours. You see, you can be anything you want to be in life. The day you were born, you came with great gifts inside of you. This is a power that no one can stop, a fire in you that no one can extinguish. That fire is what can make you become anything you want to be if you work hard, do the right thing with faith in yourself. You can be a lawyer, a doctor, a newscaster, a pilot, an actress, or an engineer. You can even become the president of your country if that is your wish. The presidential seat is meant for someone, and you are someone, so why not? Your mind is structured to accept anything it thinks. You can become anything you want in life. But it will not come easy. You will have to work hard to become that. You will meet challenges, but don't quit. I will give you one piece of advice: always have three gifts that you want to develop. You can build three careers so that if one fails, you switch to the others to make a living. It is okay to have three dreams. We live in a world with many resources to help you achieve you dreams.

The Internet, libraries, and even community centers are great resources. You can visit these places, and they are free places to search for information. How do you find out what you want to be? I have the answer for you here. First, listen to yourself, and think about one thing that you like to do all the time. Do you like doing it once you wake up, while you are eating, or while you are in school? If you like doing it all the time that is what you should focus on doing. If you like to solve math problems, then you could do well in engineering. If you like to speak in public, then you could become a motivational speaker like me. If you want to sing, may be you will become the next Beyoncé or Usher. If you like to preach, maybe you'll be the next T. D. Jakes. If you like politics, maybe you will be the next president of your country. Do you get it now? Decide what you want to be in the future, and work hard toward it. The reason I wrote this book is to help you find your calling: that which you were born to do in this life to be successful. I know that after reading this book, you will be motivated to choose a calling and work toward it.

It's easy to be frustrated with life, and you may want to give up. That's how life is. It is never easy, but only the tough will make it. Do not depend on luck to achieve things. Think about it this way: if you do not prepare for an examination but think you can pass by luck without studying, no way. You will fail.

To achieve anything, you must work hard. You have to give up many things and focus on your studies and every other thing you need to do to achieve your goals. In my journey so far, I have one major secret I used to upgrade my life every year, and I will share it with you now: I avoid people who do not encourage me. Anyone who does not encourage you to be better has to leave your life. I call them negative people. They come with all sorts of rubbish and form to distract you from doing the right thing. So watch out for them. They are bad influences, are not good, and will not teach you anything good. Make friends with people who will teach you new things. You have a right to choose your friends and terminate any relationship. It is your life, and you decide how to live it.

To achieve big things in life, you have to be firm with people. You have to know when to stop people from distracting you. Can you be a doctor? Yes, you can. Can you be a surgeon? Yes, you can. Can you be a nurse or a pilot? Of course, you can. But you have to be focused and do the hard work involved to make it happen. It will not come easy. It will come not by luck but by determination. Remember this book is about preparing you for success in the future, which is where you will live the rest of your life. That's why I wrote this book for you with love and all my energy.

Another thing you have to do to be successful is obey the laws of the land. There are laws in every school, every church, every country, and even in every family. If you break these laws, you may get into trouble. So to achieve great things you must obey the law. If you break the law, it goes on your record and may affect you adversely in the future. If you hit someone, you'll likely be in trouble. If you destroy property, that is breaking the law. Obey the law. If you disobey the law, enjoy the ride in the back of the police car. You don't want to be there, right? So avoid breaking the law so that you can be able to achieve the things you want in your life.

Avoid peer pressure, and say no to friends who are not cheering to success. It is easy to say, "I want to be successful in life." Everyone says that, but only a few work hard enough to make it. It takes hard work to be successful. You must develop a habit of never giving up. Success never comes easily, but if you continue working hard and doing the right things without giving up, your dreams will come true. Look at the lives of boxers. They make good money, but they work hard. Look at football players; they also make good money, but they really work hard. Think about the professional basketball players. They are rich, but they work very hard for their money. Doctors work hard. Look at Dr. Oz, he works very hard. Lawyers work hard too. So it's okay to admire their success, but it is also okay to feel the pain they went through to achieve what they have achieved.

I love to do things that inspire others. I love to set the pace of greatness. I love inspiration. But my inspiration doesn't come to me. I don't wait for it to come. I go out looking for it, and most times, I find it. That's why I am able to do the things I do. I feel happy sharing these things with you to inspire you to look for inspiration, because you will find it. Once you do, do not wait at all—work on it right away. That's how to be creative. School may be tough. You may hate school, but you need school to be a better person. There are no two ways about it. To do well in life, you have to do well in school. That is where to start. If you don't do well in school now, it may affect your life later, and you will regret it. No matter how much you may hate school, education will help make you a better person later in life.

Education can make you a great person in society. Go to school. Listen to your teachers. Do your homework—even do some for extra credits. That way, you'll learn more and get good grades, which will help you a lot during college admissions. Your future starts today, so start building it today. Take school very seriously, because it sets your pace for great things if only you pay attention and work hard. The time to do it is now.

One key to achieving anything you want in life is to have a big goal that challenges you. Start thinking now about the career you have to choose. I am so grateful to have visited many schools to talk to students about choosing careers. Start thinking about your career now. This career will be your job for the rest of your life, so take it very seriously. If you challenge yourself, you will be amazed at how much you can achieve. You can be anything you want, but you must challenge yourself and work hard to achieve it.

Stay around people who support you and believe that you can achieve great things. Start a hobby, like singing, playing harmonica, dancing, or even playing any sport you like. You never know if that will be a second profession for you. You may like it so much that your hobby may become your profession. Stay focused on achieving what you love, and believe it with all your heart. Enjoy your youth. You are young for only a very short period, so make use of this time to do the right things, and enjoy what you do.

To succeed in life, you have to focus on the important things. Stop searching for faults in people, and do not say bad things about them. Do not hold grudges, never be mean, and don't bully. These things take away the energy that you can put into working to make your life better. Show love and kindness, and be good to people. If you don't have anything nice to say, just keep your mouth zipped. Negativity is poison to the body, so keep away from negative things and people. Let others say whatever they want about you. Do not reply to them; rather, stay positive, and keep spreading good energy, love, and kindness, because that is what will make you a better person, and it will also change the world, which is already infested with anger, jealousy, and war. Stay focused on doing the right things. Remember, you can be anything you want to be only if you work hard and apply all of the principles in this book.

### Success Story

Steve Harvey (I am sure you know him) is always on TV. While he was in school, one of his teachers asked him what he wanted to be when he grew up. He said he wanted to be on TV. The never believed him. But Steve Harvey had faith in himself and in what he wanted to be. Several years later, Steve Harvey is not only on TV but he is on almost every major national television channel. How did he land on TV? Because he said he wanted to be on TV, believed it, and he worked hard and never let anyone talk him out of that dream.

Justin Bieber took his singing hobby to the next level to become an international sensation. You can do the same thing, but only if you believe it and work hard without letting anyone talk you out of it, not even your parents.

## A QUOTE TO INSPIRE YOU

*"Education is the most powerful weapon which you can use to change the world."*

- NELSON MANDELA

## Exercise for Building Success

Write down eight things you know you have the talent for and can develop into a career in your life. Write down what you will do to make each one possible.

1.
2.
3.
4.
5.
6.
7.
8.

# MY SIXTY POSITIVE STATEMENTS
## FOR SUCCESS

I created these positive statements to empower you and to remind you that you can achieve great things. Pronounced words have power. They're creative. Read these statements every day with the belief that they are happening in your life. Over time, they will become part of you, and help re-shape your life and future.

Now start declaring your future:

1. I was born a great kid, a star, a success, with beautiful future.
2. I am determined to succeed in life.
3. Nothing will stop me from graduating college.
4. Life is a blessing, and I am making the best use of it.
5. I don't care what others have. I am content with what I have.
6. I am strong and working toward my dreams daily.
7. I exercise three times a week, because it is good for my health.

8. Barack Obama is the first black president of The United States. I am inspired.
9. I am grateful for life, food, the air I breathe, and my teachers.
10. I am focused on achieving great things.
11. I know education is very important, so I will get it.
12. I will go to college by any good means possible for a better life.
13. I am working hard daily to achieve big things in life.
14. I have great talents. I am using them maximally.
15. Nobody can give me names that don't suit me.
16. I won't let people talk me down or tell me I can't amount to anything.
17. I am powerful, smart, and determined to succeed.
18. I am a force for creativity.
19. I learn fast and will use that skill to improve myself daily.
20. I will never be late with my homework anymore.
21. I am strong, and unique in my own standards.
22. I have many things to learn, so there is no time to hang out on the streets.
23. I love myself the way I am. That's how I was created.
24. I know lessons taught in school will change my life, so I learn them well.
25. I am created to do great things in my life and I will do just that.
26. My future is bright, and I am working hard toward it.
27. I strongly believe in myself and in whatever I do.
28. Challenges may come my way, but I always overcome them.
29. Opportunities are everywhere. I believe in possibilities.
30. I am talented.
31. I believe in doing big things.
32. Determination creates success. I am determined to succeed.
33. Eating healthy is good. I stay away from drugs and alcohol.
34. My family loves me the way I was created. I am proud of that.

35. I am special. Yes, I am.
36. I think positively all the time.
37. I am in this world to be a blessing to others.
38. I volunteer in my community. I give back.
39. Life is good, and I must do good in life.
40. I am very grateful for the blessings I have now.
41. I work hard to reach my goals.
42. I love miracles, and they happen to me every day.
43. I study hard to pass with flying colors.
44. I will learn one new sport this year and be very good at it.
45. I win all the time. I am a winner.
46. I am (your name here). I am a great person, and I know it.
47. I love myself, I love my family, and I love my country.
48. Let there be more peace in the world. I am playing my part.
49. I know good education will change my life for good.
50. My teachers are awesome, and I have a great support structure.
51. I don't want to look like anyone but myself.
52. I matter in this world, and I know it.
53. If I fail, I stand up right away and try again.
54. When I believe it, work hard, I achieve it.
55. Dreams do come true. I know it.
56. I was born to stand out.
57. I am myself, so I don't compare myself with anyone.
58. I am a gift to humanity.
59. I carry power and I know it.
60. Every day is a gift, so I receive a gift every day.

# ABOUT THE AUTHOR

 Azuka Zuke grew up in Nigeria, West Africa, and later moved to the United States. He writes self-development books, and travels, motivating people to live their dreams. He also likes taking selfies to promote unity, ignite friendship, and foster togetherness. He uses selfies to put smiles on people's faces, reduce stress, and instill a sense of oneness across all races.

Azuka, a Beverly Hills Book Award Winner is a fire-brand motivational speaker who inspires people to follow their passion and make positive changes to their lives. He is a positive thinker, a strong believer in the American Dream, a disciple of the movement for positive change and gratitude. An in-demand speaker, he passionately motivates his audience to constantly take actions and speaks with high intense energy.

Azuka is always under construction and believes in achieving great things with faith in the power and goodness of the Most High.

# CONTACT THE AUTHOR

Azuka can be reached using the following media:

E-mail: azukazuke@gmail.com

Facebook: facebook.com/Author Zuke Azuka

Twitter: @zubby34

Instagram: @authorazuka

Website: www.AzukaZuke.com

# MOTIVATIONAL SPEAKING

I am a motivational speaker.  I travel the world, speaking, motivating and empowering people to live their dreams.
For bookings, e-mail Azuka at azukazuke@gmail.com.

# APPRECIATION

Thank you for reading my book. Please share this book with your friends and your friends' friends. Knowledge is better when shared. Hopefully, I'll meet you someday, and you'll say to me, "I read your book and learned a lot."

# OTHER PUBLISHED BOOKS
# BY AZUKA

*The 9 Power Principles for Change*
*The Positive Change*
*The Power to Excel*

These books are available on Amazon.com, BN.com, and many other online bookstores in paperback form. They're also available as e-books in the Kindle store and as audiobooks on Amazon.com, on Audible.com, and in the Apple iTunes store.

Tell everyone you meet about these books.

## PUBLISHING SUMMER 2016

＝⊰⊱＝

## THE WINNER'S MINDSET
A self-development guide for young ones

# SUMMARY OF THE THINGS I LEARNED

# FROM THIS BOOK

# SUMMARY OF THE THINGS I LEARNED

# FROM THIS BOOK

# SUMMARY OF THE THINGS I LEARNED

# FROM THIS BOOK

# THE 8 SUCCESS SECRETS FOR TEENS AND YOUNG ADULTS

1. A GOOD START- will help build solid foundation.
2. LISTEN TO YOUR PARENTS AND SENIORS- it makes you humble.
3. WORK VERY HARD- it pays you back with success.
4. SHARPEN YOUR MORAL VALUES- to improve your life.
5. GET DAILY EXERCISE- for optimal health.
6. BE NICE TO PEOPLE—VOLUNTEER, it's the right thing to do.
7. BE THANKFUL EVERY DAY- it makes you happy.
8. YOU CAN BE ANYTHING YOU WANT- BELIEVE IT, yes you can for the mind is powerful.

29406529R00064

Made in the USA
Middletown, DE
18 February 2016